LOVE, THE MAGICIAN

Medbh McGuckian

LOVE, THE MAGICIAN

ARLEN
HOUSE

Love, the Magician

is published in 2018 by
ARLEN HOUSE
42 Grange Abbey Road
Baldoyle, Dublin 13, Ireland
Phone: 00 353 85 7695597
arlenhouse@gmail.com
arlenhouse.blogspot.com

Distributed internationally by
SYRACUSE UNIVERSITY PRESS
621 Skytop Road, Suite 110
Syracuse, NY 13244–5290
Phone: 315–443–5534
Fax: 315–443–5545
supress@syr.edu
syracuseuniversitypress.syr.edu

978–1–85132–192–6, *paperback*
978–1–85132–193–3, *limited edition, signed and numbered hardback*

Cover painting 'Tumbled' by Pauline Bewick
is reproduced courtesy of the artist
www.paulinebewick.ie

LOTTERY FUNDED

CONTENTS

ACKNOWLEDGEMENTS

We acknowledge the editors of journals and books where many of these poems were previously published.

Many thanks to Pauline Bewick for her beautiful cover painting.

Some of these poems were inspired by found sources. Please see the author's homepage at Queen's University Belfast for further information.

in memory of my brother
John McCaughan
1955–2014

Woman, whose elements are fire and water in the hermetic cult, is said to be in close contact with the motive-transforming agents of the universe. To love then is to be through her closer to the magical power ...

... he pre-empted a surrealist understanding of woman as an inherently magical being ...

– Anna Balakian on Éliphas Lévi

Love, the Magician

I have the feeling of being touched out
by hands as hard as wood, my insufficient
milk overwhelmingly white in this peeling
gold-vanilla centrefold. Slow and fast colours
of the black city leave embossed prints
of shadows cast by world-wide October light,
where two hills next the sea form a heart
of comely streets wharfed with worldly industry.

I think how infants sleep across the globe, the bio-
underclass, how they wear their babies to improve
the latch, of watery foremilk and creamy hindmilk
before the true milk comes in. The dust
that undergirds, collecting on their bodies,
is answered by my dark-red audience, the leaves.

The Extremely Young Age of All Seafloor
for Eavan Boland

You can tell that the sky is from
another day: apple and leaf are bringing
gaudy colours out of the sunlight, so
drawing out the Gospel marrow.

Of roses you are rose, though you did not
watch for the last of me, but touched
one button of his twice after another
if only for the beauty of their flames.

That 'soon' turned out to be leafed into
loops of full-blown, sunset-coloured roses
wrapped in the shell of a church where often
I let myself in, so safe and dull.

What could make a goddess ever cool the world
once a year, a sonnet in ivory, an ode
to desertification, a poem entered for
the marzipan prize, from there to Thankful

where her name means midday? Sometimes
I chanted the Ordinary of the Mass,
initial D with the Three Marys at the Tomb,
but never mourned for sins, *as* sins, before.

And why these gods and not others?
It's time for acts of completion,
for that green sometimes seen at the stem
end of a pineapple when the other end has faded:

for those nectar sippers, moonstone elderberries
that catch the cosmic shine like a breast
ornament rubbed with silk and amberised
as if you were brought to bed, today, of a daughter.

FROM A YOUNG GIRL TO AN OLD WOMAN

Yesterday's words have too much is
for the kiss of one field with another.
There are still letters done up
in the tailfeathers of back hair,
and acute scenes damp on eyes
like shadows within pearls ...

And everywhere else feels nearer
than England, though I like my land-poor
province as our youngest protectorate –
it wades over to me in the general
shipboard atmosphere, in immense pale
darns as though I were the one who is home.

Faithful as rain with its senses open,
its deep, earthy colour puts a well of silky
fins around the house. The lean triangle
of its head is down and governed, while its second
head inside its head (the head in its head)
gets up hungry from the conversation, goes unfed.

Yet I kiss it as my bread, this life of my land,
with its rainlilies, bloodroot, golden poppies,
its skeleton army like a family of bluebells,
its half-words or words which have never really
been born, its noises like flag-parading clouds,
its shells roofing the bay.

The street watches it as the spirit
of the street, and listens with its eyes that do not hear
the stations cried by my return ticket or
my journey money or my saved time, my wet
motor veil wing shifting to the other leg
of the H at the S and L of its mouth.

But from my breastpin a bouquet of leaves
sends my voice three fields off
across the dotted line of a road in its infancy,
a shortarm in a mirror search, to make a fragrant zone
for its swollen hands like carving,
for the camera-ready key it refuses.

STARVEGOOSE WOOD

I constructed an upsidedown garden,
one filled with the earth of Jerusalem.
The rooted addresses of the fragments themselves
have to suffocate their ripping chrysalis
like dreams which gear and unlock,
like stored snows clouded with clouds.

My elderly material pretends to be able.
My r's from the other end of Europe
say, we are from-here people, cascading
clockwork cabbages in low-earth orbit,
dying words haunting dead till the raided
cries like a three-year-old touch-deprived child.

NUMEN ADEST
for Mary McAleese

The game of light had structured her
into a town ultra-red just north
of the elbow: where the Atlantic slopes
its blue edging to the earth.
A sand glacier engulfed her
like a house where there is no Joseph.

Now as the sun is strengthened in the names
and a star takes pleasure in the kiss
which should be in the air,
the light is something expected
by a comfortable landscape
whose strict halo has loosened into classic folds.

And I, passing through a continuous
orchard, join up with its language
without taking it as my starting-point,
and let my hungriest sense be enchanted
by the interlacing sounds.

The angels of shade are twice as bright
as the innermost angels, the angel of the hour
is the angel of summer. And why am I amazed
at the angel's service? She appears
as a season of the year.

The Star Parasite

My thought became a kind of algebra
where the X sank to the bottom
as your arms submerged
into more like a pure V.
The brown rectangle and warmer browns
of your raised and squared-off arms,
drenched with an inner glowing,
reversed the typed B.

Geometic ghost, you clasped your hands
at a certain distance from my nipple
that nailed itself to your chest
as clearly as your wedded face.
The round bee-stung lips of the wine glass
opened their splendid dead-ends
to your black tongue's nocturnal squares
like a shapeless town, poorly explored.

The imaginary triangle of your Ionian
torso overlapped the real, angel-sealed
diamond of my smaller breast,
and the almonds of your thighs
arched me from the second foot
into a kneeling woman, standing woman,
crouching woman, using the same curves
to frame an arch of trees in the late forest.

Complete tree, furrowed with big veins,
I weighed you on the floor
like the drop-leaf of a table
before the shape is finally reached.
My breasts were repeated twice,
once as a sloping melon slice,
an immaterial gleam of light
whose pathway may be closed or narrowed.

And once as the brown-tipped steeper
cone, commonly found only
in young girls. They read to me
like shells on an antique piano
or a violin alongside an anchor,
stranger to me in their nudity,
forever decaying and undiscoverable
as the street incision and its surface.

The wall seemed to swing backwards,
threadlike through the increasing shallowness
of the pedestal fruitbowl, through everything
that makes a place the same place,
so what had no place
was at home everywhere.
Your fingers deadened, one after the other,
vivid and mingled, on your calf and kneecap.

You marked off their divisions, grouping
their muscles and bones like banished elements,
like teardrops repeated over and over
or a language with only one word.
And set them on your thorax,
abandoned, like one of your senses,
your gaze stepping down your share
of the house, its suggestion of hips and eyes.

NOTES FROM BED

Isabel sighs and mutters,
'This is a very Asian size.'

She feels like her whole self
is not present, when she is
acting well – she discusses
the thinking behind
the sites on the Web,
the internal representation
of your own outer appearance.

It is understandable
that all will not go smoothly.
How astonishing, when the lights
of health go down,
a returning shimmer
of who she had been.
I ask her not to use
perfumes or other scented products.

These days I don't journal.
I don't hear or speak well,
I stagger a lot, but I am not drunk.
Talk, and then I don't have to
be there, I think I gained the multiples
to help me stay alive.

If you ask me how long
I can live with my heart
the way it is, I honestly
don't know – estimating
the length of remaining
quality time – I came here
for more questions?

If I didn't have to sleep
it would be fine – it would
be all laughs. It's hard,
because I was always a fast person,
everybody knew I didn't like
going upstairs.

The sun rises again and again,
it makes one voice in my head
really clear – I would open my eyes
to the ceiling rotating in swinging arcs
around me. It slowly reaches the point
of flame, it would mean
I would receive a bona fide
mushy birthday card.

I've been told to try bee-stings,
that the ideal body is able
to get well, life may be other
than that which is foreshadowed.
The tree lives at a pace which comforts
me, my faith-based strategies
in all the sayings which he
supposedly uttered.

On both sides of the border northern flowers publish.
On the south side of a tree beneath a cinnamon-bird's
spice-built nest, the angel with the unkissed breasts
from the Annunciation on the Banks changes poses.

Quick shove of an oar, quickly corseted aneurisms
in the poems: my simple, old, old friend hands me
a bottleneck of consonants on a spade with sand.

A birdcatcher with a dish of oil, for you to look
at your own reflection, would put a jewelled feather
through your nostrils, black flyer, white raven,
duck-killer, hare-killer, fawn-killer, slow-footed goatsucker.

You are musical, a mimic, but your claws are weak,
you use a bat's wing like a baptismal icon to keep away
ants, and never stray far from the river. I have never
once met with you on the wing, your curious rolling
flight, as though your wing were hurt – a lonely bird,

cliff-martin, wolfbird, with monotonous song.
Your large eyes arrive in autumn, your exquisite sense
of blossom-headed smell; the sight of you is said
to cure jaundice, slipped below the headwaters
of the eyelid (the bird infecting itself, through the eyes).

THE MARINA OF THE BEDROOM-CARRYING BOATS

Some women, some forms of excarnation,
were called the rising of the water
when the river, after paying its visits with a deadline,
returned to its normal bed.

Where you sailed, a sea is being farmed,
summer figs from winter figs, a pair
of girl's full-size shoes from willow oars.
(An answer can grow on you fast).

In the deep midnight I play
with a twelfth of the daylight,
a complicated bird bone, mainly blue
and lilac, camel-grey.

THE BY-THE-WIND SAILOR

Think of people walking in and out
between the breathings of a world
that is a cousin to reality,
blessed household of countenances.

If I could only use these phantoms
and skip the day twenty years hence
when you abandon the mind by which
you abandon everything –

mirage, wisps of smoke, fireflies,
glowing lamp, white appearance,
red increase, black attainment.
The overthought and the underthought

of the summer headlines and my winter
rings, begged me to think again where
thoughts, if any, can be cared for,

and pasted the meaning
on the morphing sky
of the light I had shed that morning.

Prithee, unpin me.
All movement lays us bare,
of the sage-coloured cloak,
the tawny velvet cape,
the breast-cloth,
the transparent apron.

The blue god
is kissing spines
with the shoulder-blades of God.
Her lying-in girdle
and fine bearing-sheet
were sewn with a human bone
needle for making sails.

A quarter of an angel
means an indulgence
of 26,000 years
and 30 days.

The harbour is mulberry where she is still
sunk in the sleep of wordliness, visiting
herself on me, and I can no longer shut
myself off in my room as I used to.

This is the third time I have returned to earth
where I remember the room more than the life,
how my back's steel hardware broke
to shatter my inner sovereignity.

Spasms – who knew I would miss them?
Some simply exist on the gold and silver
farmland of my tongue. I felt two things
like butterflies in my secret parts.

These marks, it was believed, could come and go.
We cannot save hummingbirds unless
they have financial value. A pinch
of active bone cells and my own face

seemed to contain all its blood plus his.
He stated he had seen Temperance Lloyd
crumbling clay pictures, keeping spirits
in a wool-filled pitcher under stairs.

But she denied having allowed Scathan her cat
to suck her blood: if the imps were made
of spirit, why did the witches feed them?
And nurse them with their activated software?

The fact that I no longer fly
is my true dowry, the deep pantry
of the less and less hereafter, the love-miles
of Jesusa, the car-parking angel.

THE MARCELLA QUILT

Dear one, you never wet the tea,
after a day a-shopping for caps and gauzes
among smirking mercers and finical man-milliners
at the Fan and Pepper-Box in Drury Lane.

In my plain white, tie-on pocket
ornamenting the area at my waist,
my stomacher, the locket with my mother's hair
(*mon coeur est à toi*),

the rose pin, the pebble brooch, the night
earrings. Could I not meet
with a necklace such as Lady Betty
desired, ready-strung? They make none

but with drops and young serpents
hanging in curls. Cards half-burnt in the grate
in return for her honour
suggest temper and despair.

A dated invoice lies in one corner
of her reticule. I was so vex'd,
I borrowed my Lady Sunderland's
jewels and made a tearing show.

I bit a piece of my fan out,
not knowing what I did,
like a proud little hussy
with a round-frock on.

We are what we borrow:
for her to whisht, you sowbelly,
and the whites of his pious eyeballs
swering her to silence and coort.

DEAR MADAM NINE

Let your side-glass down hastily, if a spotted woman
masked like a covered dish, side-glass you again,
for fear of her not being wholesome. She seems
very much inclined to a decay and succumbs
to the vapours in a plain undress cap, he had
absolutely made love to her square-cornered
heart and her scarlet trimmed nipples, despite
the hush-hush of your prior claim to him.

With her decreasing face and increasing waist,
her book is spoiling good conversation in Dublin
where all the Misses are writing plays.

Her jewels out of pawn, she will see you
past the gander, at the Blue Peruke,
on the Strand, next door to The Cocoa Tree.

Lurgy Brack Down Hazel
To my Negro wench Silla, one of the scabbiest whores, and all her breed

A freshly-collected memory pauses
like a kind of blush upon the nebula.
The heavy near light is as far as their
distance down the corridor from my office.

The old new river is a misfit, its bedload
too large for its valley. New seeds need
to be entered, vaguely Christian child-
naming ways in a small, small town.

On white sky days, first person warnings
from the dead travel over my mind
to puff their vendible poetry. My unmortified
state is a slow-growing mountain.

There are vapoury disorders from the rain skin
on the meadow roof, from the bitter wood
in the intelligent blinds. The all-important
mouth-feel is prideful, never once mentioned

                    the word 'love'.

Jane Anger, thou art a whore
and an arrant whore and a common
carted whore. Go, go, Magdalena,
thou art a base beggarly queane
and not fit to dwell in such a place
as this amongst honest neighbours,
but in some out place or back lane
amongst such as thyself art.

Sicilia Spicer, Helena True, Rebecca Askew,
you might have learned to read but not
to write. Thou dost carry a box of complexion
about thee, Lucretia Treat, Elizabeth Clay,
thou keepest privat knaves in thy house
or else thy bed would not go jig and jog
so often as it doth. Thou didst offer to give
me an angel of gold to occupy me.

Isabel South, Winifred Bland, Margery
Hipwell, thou didst break thy glass windows
and kept a noise of fiddlers all
night in thy shop. Emma Bacchus, Susan
Lark, thou art a drab and a harlot,
I would cut thee as small as herbs
to the pot, thou art a wrymouth queane,
thou art beggarly descended.

Margaret Wild, Mary Sadd, Rhoda
Greenrise, it was long of Alice Moody
that I lay bedrid thereon.
I am not so scurvy a woman as you
for I never sold my daughter's maiden
head. Alas, poor ninny horner he,
he hath given her that, that will stick
by her for forty weeks.

Katherine Fairmanners, Rachel Sharp,
thou art a hospital whore and St Katherine's
whore. If thou art not with child,
yet thou hast deserved for it.
A child thou hadst, and a child thou hast
made away. I will keep reckoning for thee,
and thou shalt be delivered of *that* child
a month before Christmas next.

Aveline Shepherd, Frances Sweeting,
I am past twice seven yeares old, and
God forgive me if I think amiss, I wish
your good, I speak not all that I could speak.
I never carried a pair of sheets out of doors
for a Holland smock. A cart and a basin,
ting, ting, if thou wilt not be quiet. Had I
any more law than an honest woman should have?

Sage Povey, Ann Bird, she has used her pleasure
of me in speeches, she is a creature
that had need to be twice defined.
Nothing desired she more than to give
affronts in public places. Her imperious tongue
runs descant on every subject ministered.
And now she waxeth old,
she will turn bawd.

Her son swept dust into my child's face
in a yard at Coldharbour,
in the summer of 1614. He found
the rhyme embroidered on a bridge
and carried it back to his alehouse
where I dress the wholesome diet,
and drink to you, and all the malice
I bear to you, I put in this glass.

The question mark turns like a fishhook:
such a one ought to be naturally
of a sweet and virtuous disposition.
She ought to be between 20 and 30 years of age,
to have lain-in a little before the child's mother, an honest
woman, such as had a man child last afore, nor
approaching near unto her time again,
free also from the scurvy, scabs or hard glands,
as these are indications that her humours are corrupted.

A fat nurse is preferable to a thin one, but if one can be
found that nearly corresponds with the constitution
of the child's mother, she will answer still better:
she ought to be able to suckle at each breast,
the nipples of which should be of a middling size.
These ought also to be irritable, so they grow erect
by being gently stroked with your finger,
which is a necessary quality of their giving milk.

Whose goodness may be tried,
    1: by its colour, which ought to be rather bluish.
    2: by the smell, as it should be void of any.
    3: by the taste, not by any means salt or bitter.
    4: by its consistence, when thin it is always better
        than thick.
    Therefore a drop of it on your nail, ought easily to run off
    on inclining it. Even on shaking the finger hastily,
    there ought not to remain the least white streak on
    your nail. That milk is good, which neither fletheth
    abroad at every stiring, nor will hang fast when you
    turn it downward, but that which is between both is best,
    5: by the touch, because not any pain ought to be felt,
    on letting a drop of it fall into the eye.
    6: with rennet, for if the milk gives much cheese,
    you may judge it to be good for nothing.

7: by keeping it several hours in a glass, if it gives much cream, it will also prove bad, the lighter it will be found.

8: by the age, because the older the milk, the more unhealthy it will be.

She should have a large and airy chamber, tolerably kept warm, as also to prevent the nurse and child from getting the itch.

Except when it cannot be avoided, she ought always to cover her breasts very well: small beer may be drank at pleasure, so that she may accustom the child unto mirth, but neither sour, new, nor stale, and not by any means, when drawn overnight – wine, brandy, ale or coffee ought by no means to be given her.

White coral increases the supply.

Do you insist upon a certain region?

No, provided that she's not from Lorraine.

If the nurse be squint-eyed, she cannot look upon the child but side ways. They say that Michelangelo was nursed by a stonemason's wife. That the royal prince has one each night in rotation, one for suckling, rocking, holding and walking.

He was nursed by an Irish nurse, after the Irish manner, where they put the child into a pendulous satchel instead of a cradle, with a slit for the child's head to peep out.

For there are some who –
unutterable though it is to say –
have Christian nurses whom they
do not permit to feed
their children when they have
eaten the body of Christ

which descends through bodily processes,
unless for three days beforehand
they express their milk into the latrine.

At the appropriate time, let the teat be anointed
as with aloes, or wormwood, or mustard,
or soot steeped in water. The way Licidas rushes
to see if you have milk, it would seem the rake
is interested in the baby. His mother came to see him
with her cousin with the moustache, and I would bet,
Philis, that he has fathered it.

THE CHARACTER OF THE DUG EXPLAINED

Philosophy I say and call it he, my throat hurts
from all the j's and h's: a woman and a melon
are both alike, nobody knows what is in them
until they are broke up. It is as impossible
to dive into the heart of a woman as to run
your head, body and all into her fundament.

You have taught the curious sight to press
into the privatest recess of her littleness,
her sweet-bread, piss-bladder, arse-gut,
flank-bone, the parts which in women serve
for generation, the descendant trunk
of Vera Cava with its branchings,
the trumpets of the womb or blind passage
of the seeds, resembling the wings of bats
or flittermice, the greatest and middlemost kernel.

A thing so sealike, so investigable, that no chart
can direct us – men use to look for wine where
there is a bush, and a good inn hath very seldom
a bad sign-post. But some women are nothing less
than what they most appear, as if they were
created for no other end than to dedicate
the first-fruits of their morning to their looking-glass
and the remainder thereof to the playhouse.

As it is no imperfection in the hare to be fearful
or the tiger to be cruel, they have a whole arsenal
of aspects and idle looks, gaudiness and ceremonies.
They will wanton with their gloves and handkerchiefs,
thrust out their breech or bite their lips
like a nimble frigate before a fresh gale.

Who knows whether a merry humour
be a testimony of looseness or freedom

between a strange woman and a woman
that fears the Lord?

A clean-limbed wench that has neither spavin, splinter,
nor wind-gall, may have little hard breasts
and a round chin that denotes envy, her small mouth a
sign of weakness and lying, her long neck a timorous
disposition and a person inclined to loquacity. She could
not possibly carry herself in a worse way than she does,
discovering all her cunning knacks and facts.
How wittily she doth bestow her cheats, so to manage
her wit, as if she were at a prize.

These are absolute symptoms, whose seeming purity
is made strict by the power of drugs: women who use fard
are trifling and full of tattle, they would obtrude
on the underwits, whereas the wise sort of people
know this almost for a maxim, Poeta Nascitur, Non Fit.
No, they should go to their black velvet caps
and chains and ruffs, as it was in my time.

Imoinda Birthing

We sleeping volcanoes are tender, thoughtful,
suffering, but not endlessly.
All that about having your skirt to the floor,
when leaves are already lifted
just prior to the onset of dawn.

Seasonal tilting, shading of wings,
October was one of the few things
that arrived in the time being.

To make privacy your mind's melody,
to leave oneself behind violently,
swim to the light, to infinity plus,
solitary hunter of words,

while I hold my head one way
and my hands another,
my best petticoat guarded with velvet.

THE HODEGETRIA

Our moon reflects, having no other choice,
the calm insignificance of the sea.
We won't find a soul by cutting deep
from the response of the day
or the red ink parts of the Gospel.

A woman at one with her sari
knows by instinct how to place it:
her sari is a fellow-actor, constantly
on stage. Why do we wear
such static, stitched clothing?

Already we are withdrawing
from the comfortable idea, of women
who mend roads. Her two shoulders
are touched by the garment
in different ways:

the right side of her waist is hot
from the pleats, her ankles
always feel slightly crowded,
their movement made heavier
by the fall.

It functions usefully
as a kind of third hand
for lifting vessels, cleaning, wiping,
gathering, protecting the face
like a fan in summer.

It gets jammed in a car door,
flies in your eyes or slips off your head,
you bite it between your teeth
or in your fist, you pat your lips with it,
dab with it at your tears.

You may tie the string so tightly
as to harm an unborn baby –
when breast feeding, it is a cradle,
a cloth for the baby's cheek.
He plays hide and seek with it,

sliding and showing his face.
When he sleeps he pulls it
twisted around his thumb
into his mouth – if you
disengage it, he screams.

When we lie next each other,
I wind it round me pretending I'm not there.
He learned to walk clinging
not to my finger but my sari.
Even after forty years

you never really feel command
of its rich lather, stunningly radiant
cloud. To tame and inhabit
its fearsome flood of fabric
is to be a person given the gift

of decay. The forms of pouring
what I must have ceased to be
are the unsure position of the folds
on the sari of an elderly woman
and its wilted pastels.

The Conditions of Wearing a Veil

They must not perfume themselves.
They must not wear adorning clothes.
They must not wear thin clothes.
They must not wear narrow or tight clothes.
They must cover their entire bodies.
Their clothes must not resemble men's clothes.
They must not wear sound-producing garments.
Their foot-ornaments must not produce sound.
They must not walk in the middle of streets.
If it is necessary to talk, they must talk
in a low voice, without laughter.

INNOCENT III

An owl has as good a soul as a cuckoo and I believe
that for as long as you have lived
you have never seen a soul go blackberrying.

God made the fishes and birds from the water
but he made man from the foulest and lowly earth,
from the stench of both persons in lusting.

The fetus is nourished in the womb
by the foulness of menstruation,
the flow of which ceases because of this duty.

Crops do not grow that come into contact
with menstrual matter. Orchards wither,
dogs that eat it become rabid.

Those conceived in its flow become lepers,
contract the elephantine illness,
or other hereditary diseases.

Birth is worthy of tears, because
of the ugliness and the production of groans:
in the sorrowful suffering of the newborn boy,

he cries with more force, according to his strength
and voice, saying 'A' upon leaving the womb.
The newborn girl, less strong and weaker in voice,

proclaims 'E', hence, they say E or A,
all those born of Eva. It exits the womb
with its head between its knees,

palms lying above the face.
It leaves backwards against the back
of the mother, which teaches a mystic weariness.

She who fails to guard the host carefully
and a mouse eats it
shall do penance for forty days.

But she who loses it in the church
so that a part falls and is not found,
twenty days.

She who acts with negligence towards the host
so that it dries up and is consumed by worms
until it comes to nothing
shall do penance for three forty days
or a year
on bread and water.

If it is entire, but a worm
is found in it, it shall be burned
and the ashes concealed beneath the altar.

If it loses its taste and is discoloured,
she shall keep a fast for twenty days.
If it is stuck together, for seven days.

She who wets the host shall forthwith
drink the water that was in the chrismal
and take the host and amend her fault
for ten days.

THE COMFORT STATION

A witness has said that you raped women
and brought them to the barracks to be used by the Japs.

I organised a brothel for the soldiers
and went there myself.

Were the women willing to go?
Some were willing, some not.

How many were there? Six.
How many were forced? Five.

Why were they chosen?
They were daughters of men who attacked us.

Then they were punished for the deeds of their fathers?
Yes.

How long were they kept? Eight months.
How many used them? Twenty five.

Did they bathe between the rapes?
They were lined up in threes and the twenty five soldiers
mentioned above charged them with bayonets,
killing three at a time.

CONVERTED CHURCH

I couldn't cultivate myself,
this moment has settled in my blood
to return to whatever it locked.
Watchings, lowness and melancholy.

I did manage to bottle the cherries
despite the bitterness of the honey
and the wilderness between things,
my life from inside out so peculiar.

How could it be a mistake?
How should she not flow black?
And what is a clinging street,
more alive than indoors?

It neither hurt nor didn't hurt.
The bird-headed sunboat might have tried
to extinguish itself as it left the house,
left the unchanging farmstead,

the city frozen in its past:
to the sun's mind, ruthless departure.
And though mimosas steep the bedroom,
no two hands ever forgot themselves

in birdsong like the touch of hands
when our dreams are loosened in us.
My under-the-breath prayer
has an angel-maker's church air

of modesty. Whether the name
of the illness is lilac,
radiance is the middle daughter.
Dark is the meadow,

the darkest and most meagre
blue of existence. But the moon
is ablaze in the rose-light of the sun,
waiting for the right light.

Dramatic horseshoe of beeches, whose leaves
have simply unwrapped to a fluffy garden.
Why do you feel you have been there in the past?

The house is shaking itself gently, for no reason,
and I am weary of its modulations, delicate
though they be, like a tree slowly melting,
or a maternal hand over the hair,
inhaling your silken back.

One should listen as it were, against them,
some of life's ingredients, the horseshoe
that dented somebody's head, so that
her blood poured out for his bath and her veins
were woven into a little dress for him.

The treatment last winter could not check it.
Nothing can check it now, since clouds
have inscrutable wills to swell across
the wind-thrown milky sunshine where
a lost golf ball is caught in a chaplet of bluebells.

Not till I have crossed another border
will a life arrive, though inside that grey
no heart can yet flow. Mostly untouched,
she watches the longing with which her friend
kisses the spotlighted earring, the heaven
a star is to the floor of time,

the petals bursting to the rosary,
feast-day opening of a winged altar.

SNAPDRAGON

It may be described as everybody's flower,
like an ordinary rose, choosing cloudy
weather, quite unaffected by the rain,
sunproof, with golden lip and light green
eye, flounce upon flounce, and undercolouring
of cherry, oversheen of clear, soft, old
garden cerise. When in fourth leaf,
it throws a small percentage of blue
to its nodding pale cheddar pink or pleasing
primrose companion, a shade more salmon
in the improved sunset's strongest of orange,
beautifully-netted skin; expressing not more
than five words of greetings to the young
grass (it may be meadow turf)
whose round seedlings feed off dark rays.

CALICO CAT

I understood even less today
how I have been able to house a lake
that flows day and night without stop
between the skin and the scarf skin.

There's a double movement somewhere,
something happening, something in the nature
of a sunrise – the thread must be plucked
from the very world in which it beats,

while the hawthorn meanders gorgeously
christening the trees, and the flyblown
faces of the gone look out at bright sand,
those sensed inner standing higher beings.

Snowed under by colours, the chairs add
blue afterthoughts to the twelve o'clock
light and shade. I shall never make
you black, who loved the sea whatever it did.

I have a quick ear for different people's
step, I live in puzzledom and wonder
where everything is, cannot remember
new things, the days who silently gather.

I closed his eyes myself, dull stones
set in the ring of the mixed city,
eyes which didn't open wide, it is almost
at odds with morning which is which.

We must bring the summer to ourselves,
even if the house has lost all meaning
for its owner, to become soft, melted,
able to act the one hundred word tombstone.

WAITING FOR THE WATER TO BELL

Colours are at work
re-enspiriting
this ancient autumn movement,
the winter nectar grounds.

The sky of Mars is dull ochre,
its clouds are always
beautifully arranged,
the fourfold year, full moon days,

purples and blues stretch further,
blue flowers, the rarest ones.
There is a supernatural weariness
to her body's moulded river.

One moment she looks liverish,
the next her skin is steel-grey
pearly again. She seems
to be a ghost and perhaps, is not.

It is a manner of treating leaves
when a skin is described
as velvety or a piece of lace,
the occasion of a descent of grace.

I like all pictures with
Christ in them,
much as in the past
a crucifix was kissed.

A language was never made
that I go into my mother's world,
the bowl of her eye like a berryless
stem melting light.

The crimson Jesus
followed by memory
who has eyes in the back of her head
is ruin in my breast pocket.

If I considered
this group of pale colours
as 'Christ rising',
it is a poplar, it is a storm,

a way doubtless
de-sanctified
which can be interpreted as predestined
like any kind of precious strange coincidence.

FOR PEGGY WHO STOOD FOR ME

When her 'remains' are carried
to the chapel this Sunday,
she will be the first to pay
a visit to me here,
sitting upright as at Mass
so that I don't lose sight of her
alone among the crowd
at the heel of the court.

Her eyes without a word
smiling out loud
as they lock around both of us
their gates of horn.

A Circle of Circles

Splendour, mirth and good cheer,
the wish puts them on his arm.
They build themselves out into the blue,
skated-over, carefree, bright-
dark arousing blue,
colour of distances impinging.

Nothing happens in the mirrors
of the scribbled-open dream,
but brilliant births take place
in the clan to which the night-
dream belongs.

The just-lived moment is its own
peculiar minus for one
who has finally become worldless,
even to the repose of wishes,
their incoming forwards, their bygone above.

INFORMANT; QUALIFICATION; MOTHER

Her script is very shapely,
her body still pliant and fragrant as the cloud
still over you.

Cryptic eventless decades
have flared over her freezing
an irresistible dolour
easily overlooked.

Shod in lilac, the whispered dust
curated the season.

A seagreen ribbon
of copper butterflies
cleaves the unadopted road
into the hornbeam grove.

THE FAR FETCHER

Like most uneducated Englishwomen,
I like reading books in the bulk – for whose,
whose sake? One of those
interlaced angels I had been taught to detest?

All we have to go on is the words,
the as-it-were outside, trace of the spoken
before the first sound.

The earth will drift exactly as it pleases,
natural sun and absence of stars
saying dawn and meaning twilight,
bringing into her body a future she knows
she will never have.

She is a thing in slumber, near phantom,
iceberg in the last stages of decay,
pearlware piece.

Only the seagull perched on her head
can feel the hum of her thoughts –
if she would have then
opened her mouth properly
and told me more.

WEDNESDAY SERMONETTE

This is not a merciful city –
Marine Silence Street, All
of God's Angels Church,
the Inn of the Last Nail.

As always, when I am far from you,
I am languidly contemplative
of my own phantom, her experience
of the mother me.

A year here has two seasons,
white winter and green winter,
the white lasts nine and a half months,
the green two and a half.

Now is the beginning of the green,
it has been raining continuously
for twenty-one days, and will
do so till the end.

The red-lipped apples are kept asleep
in a mottled shapeliness. A white moss
appears in the corners of the warmest
room. I live mostly in the wardrobe.

Above, the curtains glow red, bodywide,
where the tenant died in the summer.
The sight of her coat makes me feel
accompanied, at the turn towards

the world of souls in November.
She was aware now and could name it,
capable artist of the darkness,
she could tolerate my heart

like the medicine of not eating,
she increased her brow, erased a vein
in her neck, letting a hare
escape from the fold of her dress.

I hear his voice and hers,
they are returning from the garden
and it so late, the entire garden
turns orange, like a spiritual meadow.

Her body with its seatime tang
of warm pine and larch needles
was what of recent years
so deepened my poetry

and made my dark clothes
so impossible. I have got black-
edged paper to rewrite an old poem,
since there are more nows than one,

and the memory of all my alcoves
is like long vanished prayers.
I've lost the bluish colour in my hands,
my make-up lopsided or missing.

Of the three of us there were only
two of you, the one of me
is grateful for the half of you,
for strong lifesigns and smoothness of heart.

The weight of the clock burns
a spicy rosemary fire
with a gossamer rose colouration,
the essence which the moon bestows on the herbs.

The day and month windows
were also floor to ceiling windows.
I watched the trees with the same shock
as all those other leavings,
their flowered relics keeping perfect track
of my dreams. And, sleeping white,
I hoped I wouldn't stare away the afternoon,
I had never held it up to the suggestive light.

You have been inside a placid enough river,
in an underneath sort of fine aloneness.
How kind you thought your mother's window boxes
of geranium, fuschia, musk. It was as if
her faulted love nursed you in the snow,
wearing ballet slippers in the rain,
a long slow nursing where her breasts
tensed by death might simply fail to press
your fingers through her dress
that had come fresh to her body.

Though she is the eternal daughter
and you the ever-present, dark brother
or sister, whose shadow is the lighter
of the two brothers. Sweat-smelling pennyworths
of golden ointment, zinc and rosewater
embroider a sickle moon on each shoulder
where the sleep-thorn made its own cloud design.

My hand ungloved for tea, I stroke just once my desk,
wondering if I would forget your name for a moment.
Then almost wake you with my concern
at every breath rich and stolen,
at your flirting so bloodlessly
with the grey flute, blue flute dispersal lawn
and its single cement pillowcase:

The heart of a girl
will give you twice as much time to live
as the heart of a boy.

MANAGED NEWS

Melissa's eyes own and divide the day
like flowered sceptres
against an oval blue crystal.

Unwavering moonlight
on the upper part of the house,
now east, now south,
shines on her lap.

There are twelve garnets
on each arm –
in the leaf plan
of the fan-shaped lawn,

by distant caressing
inside her face,
dance and silk
come together as one.

NOIR POEM

Phantom leaf turquoisely braked
by the sitting down or getting up
of two women: at the far end,
the falling of a simple lipstick,
petals stuck to the tongue.

BASILDON BLUE

It's all, I'm afraid, downhill,
the once-flower moon being on her back
in the completely lifeless street
as good as gold as the day is long.

There was a gap in the dream
before the dream proper, the dream's extras
swanned around a table laid in the shape
of a horseshoe, eating out of the palm

of her hand. In the highly elegant
goodslift, she kissed me with great skill.
My raw silk jacket got caught
on an ochre-coloured cloud

that raced past the house
as if the dream had been wasted
by the combustion of the dream in prayer,
the Saint Francis in San Francisco.

Inevitably, I begin counting the days
alone in painted indoor forests.

The absolutely sunless house
the colour of dried rose-petals.

A veil of red silk covers the desk.
A green more dark edges the ash-green windows.

What phenic acids, what copper solutions
tenderly drawing up her furs over her shoulders.

His top hat sports two pearls, his waistcoat
tinted wine-fire-opal.

And as I button my boots with a hairpin,
his lavender-blue eyes suffuse my skull with liquid rays.

BROWNFIELD

Each of the occupants
of the anywhere building
has five lean views.
The fresh carpeting feels
exposed in the womb, offshore.

Glass, that heroic material,
opens and shuts the skies
in the low north roof,
where the new, new thing
is a blue just like the old blue.

The wear and tear of daylight
needs to be dark just at present
for soil to stretch up an inch,
for the extra blossoms to wither
whatever autumn leaves there are.

The sunweb in the centre
is a tree-lined interior,
an internal street,
with only the weaker trees,
leaving the strong mother trees

to call for a child when there is none.
That black behind the shoulder
redolent of a branch
is a rainier wind
only just not touching

not magnetic or map south
but true polar south,
and thinking, by way of a neighbour,
what does the river want,
each successive touching of the land.

The Instant of the Computer-Directed Thought

The path to my bedroom is paved with black
pills for when the seasons change as they are
doing now. This time last year the lilac covering
the light on her lips made even dreams unnecessary.

I am dragging the tip of a pen like part of a wing-
casing, hearing sounds without listening while I
am thinking. I feel the science of my life, the Madaming,
as it is called, Violet or Sugarplum, Buttercup or Lulu.

Families of clouds remote and underfoot possess
a circus of strokes at the very edge or backbone
of the white table. It's the sort of thing that happens,
the propagating, contagious, misfolding of a protein.

Suppose you could turn the cradlewomb of earth
just a little bit, for the last refuge of colour
buried alive inside its language, obliterated
by earthshine and a day of two weeks?

We hallucinated like a breast's temperature
the smell of space in the window, our banshee
jet of crushable aluminium honeycomb
a dew of black blood, soft key to the moon garden.

Whose plains named after states of mind
eventually would meet us, as wine lingered
around the chalice captured in the looser gravity
that gripped us, then pressed us into the ocean.

Eavesdrop Burial

Rain beyond rain
thought beyond thought
till no thought at all.
In the car-stricken streets
of never sun-kissed Ulster,
a fluidity of being walked on
like a word missing a Y.

A bank of sped-up clouds
scoops light into grey-moulded
cloudwater. The clouds have spines
of ice within their amber-tinged
breasts. The purplish-white sky
displays a burnished forehead,
removes her four wings and eats them.

It's that far gone, the summertime,
I never opened up my own thinking
to the self-proclaimed thief of thoughts,
my eventual self in another piece
of city, where the ruins of the future
wash up against buildings like a shore.
They shun the moonlight hanging on tree-tops,

a sprinkling of forgiveness, in which
the tree unveils the equations that govern
the rose. All I have of rich
is sliding up to notes with a sense
of winter echo. In the rise of the lane
or the flag of the fire, I too will shine
like a violet, when bogwood is thrown on.

Part of the condition is not being able to remember
the name of the condition. The secret of happiness
is to have forgotten what it is to be happy.

She knew that distance can create closeness,
having to sit with her knees drawn up to her chin,
using the lustrous fleck of her lips and slant of eyelids

to liquefy. A pure moon swung into the blue garden
where everything has plenty of time to flower twice
over, the blue lupin, the Madonna lilies, every known
rose, white dahlia after dahlia, the much Europeanized
flowers, their subtle cosmic fragrances. Carnations
on the coffin of ardent old bones, lying under the mauve

poppies. The war-sadness fell on the stone baskets
of fruit, in order to make words out of their blood.
She was kept warm from the inside by her books.

BREAKDOWN OF LETTERS

In consequence of the late sad event
in Henrietta Street, I have borne
the arrival of your pretty letter today
extremely well. A thank you for every line.

Your comfortable letter found me
at the breakfast table, soon after
I and my impatient feelings walked in.
I am writing in the yellow room,

having got up between 6 and 7.
I have really been too unwell
from my late oppression in the head
this last fortnight, to write *anything.*

I believe I drank too much wine
last night, I know not how else
to account for the shaking of my hand.
Your long letter was valued as it ought,

such a long letter, two and forty lines
in the second page. A nice, brotherly
letter, I assure you I thought it
very well worth its two and three.

It was quite as long and particular
as I could expect. I have torn
it open and read your civil note,
I read it through the very even

I received it. The novelty of it
may recommend it, it came just in time,
a medley and satisfactory letter.
I shall take care not to count

the lines of your last agreeable
composition. I had sent off
my letter yesterday before yours came,
I had no idea of hearing from you

before Tuesday. You produced an apology
for your silence, I received it with much
philanthropy and still more peculiar
good will, you write so even,

though every line was inclining too much
to the north east. I read it aloud
again by candlelight, I have nothing
but good to say of it. As to making

any adequate return for such a letter
as yours, it is absolutely impossible.
For we feel, more and more, how much
we have to do and how little time.

Nobody can desire your letters
as much as I do. I have made it
a rule not to expect them
till they come, as only one coach

comes down on Sundays. I had
thought with delight of saving you
the postage – I admired
your red wafer very much.

I take the first sheet
of this fine-striped paper.
The day seems to improve –
I wish my pen would too –

I must get a softer one.
You did not find my last letter
very full of matter, the nonsense
I have been writing, my adventures

since I wrote to you three days ago?
It was absolutely necessary
that I should have a little
fever and indisposition, you understand

enough of the whys and wherefores,
you may accordingly prepare
for my ringing the changes
of the glads and the sorrys for the rest

of the page. I eat my meals
on the sofa in a rational way.
I expect a very stupid ball,
there were only ten dances

of which I danced seven.
If there is any feeling to be had
for love or money, be it lesson
or country dance, sonata or waltz,

you are its constant theme.
Constancy – I am not afraid
of the word, I see nothing alarming
in the word, I would spell it

with anybody, since there is now
something like an engagement
between us, and the day is come
on which I am to flirt my last.

But I am getting too near
complaint, it is what you must
not depend upon ever being
repeated. I am forced to be

abusive, for want of matter.
Having really nothing to say,
from a doubt of the letters'
ever reaching you. We have been

very gay since I wrote last,
everything quite in stile, not
to mention the funeral which
we saw go past. And still more,

all in the rain. Back again,
because it rained harder,
I found my mother sitting by
the fire and certainly in no respect

worse than when I left her.
The last letter I received from you
was dated Friday the 8th.
It was chaperoned here

by a scrap from James to say
that Mary was brought to bed
last night – as to make me want
to lay in myself – I am sure

of meeting Martha at the christening.
I gained a promise of two roots
of heartease: but I think I may boast
with all possible vanity, I shall never forgive you.

THE BEDE-ROLL

To the high altar, for tithes detained
and underpaid, a book to be laid
on a lectern, on the south side of my tomb.

My body to be buried in the middle
of the aisle, at my father's head.
To an honest priest, to see my body brought

to the ground and keep my earthtyde,
sing a trental for my soul, ten shillings.
He to do for me three deeds of charity

to the poor people that shall be present
on my burial day. To the reparation
of the bell-ropes, my finest sheet,

a blue coverlet with white roses and red,
a gown trimmed with otter. To my confessor,
two pence, with two almost black calves.

To every of my children, a gold ring.
My house and the pondyard over against it
to be sold, the money thereof coming

to bring me to the earth. To the emendation
of the common way between my gate
and the stone cross, three loads of sand

to be delivered, on this side my thirty day.
My silk hat to be delivered, immediately after
my decease, to Joan Fox, with my oldest gown,

a working day kercher, my holiday kercher.
To Margery, a long chain. To Agnes, a little chest.
To Alice, my sister, my best striped gown.

To each of my godsons, two bushels of barley.
To my shepherd, ten ewes with lambs, to each
of my god daughters, a lamb.

To Robert, a close of meadow. To the same Alice
aforesaid, a brass pot, six silver spoons,
my best pan. Christian, my daughter,

to be supported with my goods till she is
twelve years old. To my cousin, my best cow.
To Ralph, a brass jug, all the kitchen

with the well. To Margaret, my kinswoman,
my green silver girdle, a bowl with a gilt rim
for salt, the best bell of my mother.

To my servant, two pewter saucers,
disposing each year in bread, ale and cheese,
for my soul. To my brother, a hosecloth of kersey,

my largest platter, my table, a pan holding
a gallon, my best bedcover, my tabard
and furred tunic, my best hood.

And so from year to year, a bullock with a flaxen
mare, a sorrel mare, a brown gelding,
my boat with the tackle to it belonging

to keep her markets, my parlour and my chamber,
with free coming and going thereto all times.
To my ghostly father, my bed complete

with all things apt and fit for a soul
to lie in. To Annabel, my ambling mare,
to ride upon the holy day to church,

three geese, a cupboard that standeth
in the hall, the form with the stained cloths,
one candlestick, a yellow kerchief, two flock beds,

my gown furred with black lamb,
my middlemost spit, a tearing apron,
a shelf that stands bare in the buttery.

To Edmund, my black mare that is bald,
my meadow that is called Wrong Meadow,
with the easement of the well, one yard

called the Field Yard, my ploughs and my harrows,
all the timber that is about my ground,
land which a single oxen could till

in one year, a bullock called Young Mother,
a milch cow, forty shillings
of lawful money of England.

My Chaise

My corpse in a hearse and six horses.
Immediately following it my chaise and four
driven by my own coachman and postilion
in black jackets, and the glasses of my chaise
down to show it empty.

My three footmen and grooms
two on each side my chaise, in black jackets
made in the same form as their riding jackets.
Two coaches and six to follow my chaise.

I desire the black plumes and velvet
may look fresh and good
and that the black hatbands and gloves
be also good.

I desire no escutcheons
or any show whatsoever,
my chaise will show who it is.

The Short Journey of his Lips

Lower the gap-ringed, split-red sun
adrift in a two-pointed flame
into its beclouded terrace of anger.
The soul will slowly burn
its born-lover remembrance of itself.

Its patches of father-tone, apparently
seamless red couplets, bloodsisters
of the stove-god who collapses
at home. You may glimpse a saddle

folded back into the flow
if you swear dry kinship
in the overcrowding of those poems
with one of the tenderest mountains.

LOVE, THE MAGICIAN

Another well-loved wreck in the vicinity:
snow-rigged, the others, nothing, gone.
The motionless twilight is death personified,
two cold shoulders, his distant ghostly form.

Such a faraway dance of black sounds,
it surprises Persia. The swiftly-wasted seconds
of his moving mouth and larynx
are smothered objects in the demolition

of his spine. They expect a world
like the one they abandoned, once
you've arrived, it matters little
how you've arrived there. He's

no more like himself than his carcass,
though it seemed that a carcass
was worth having, since it is placed
as a hinge. There is no exactly,

the comparative pallor bringing it
too home, the need to shut a meaning
out. His third sister, I distressed
the paint surfaces on the path

of accompaniment, living and the sound
of it, a face their lovers would hardly
know pleads to be seen once more.
His eyes were fixed on the fig tree

or a spider's web, the light was such
as oft in a woodland. Young moonlight
began to touch words with new measures
of touch: his balloon prospect,

his sky-situated knowledge: this
is how I am, this is how it was.
To watch this unguarded sleep
is the end of old poems, is to settle

in the most remote of fountains.
Death? It is not as interesting
as the orgasmic aspect of the weather,
the apple-cheeked river, the yellow rose

that ought to be red. You pull
the rope of your door tighter,
you seem almost folded in two
by the embrace of the ground

whose horizon will act as a brake.
I desired my dust to be mingled
with yours, when the eternal comes
over me, when we have got over

the rolling banner of texts
and the strangeness of the veiled late.
The moss caulking remains frustratingly
mute, silt lies thick inside the hull,

but water so blessed must hold
something marvellous – your courage
so high it was all over the heavens,
it became a universe.

Till my soul overpass,
through such a block of reality,
in till the hill like a sparrow,
waking, he meets the shepherd.

SEEING TESS

The house's bulky shapes,
I was all they,
the world and sometimes his wife
rubbing each other into wounds.

Swathes of housing
of almost quaint perfection
gathered on the candles
in a clear and delicate
enlarged stream.

A gourd came up in the night
and cast its shadow over my head
leaving behind the germ
of an Iseult poem.

I have never had breakfast
in that small smoking room,
in search of cobwebs
on the coral eiderdown
over the desk of his life.

A Prayer for Carnal Delectation

The light proves that he is reading still.
Cover the little Indian boat on the mantelpiece
with a black cloth, or an orange cloth,
or both, to be mystical to the point
of absurdity. Like snow.

The owner drew a cross through
this golden up-to-date little prayer,
and now she sleeps in her own character
who took complete control of your lips
and kneaded the moon into the shape
of your head, to learn a larger breath.

YEATS'S FISHERMAN, CHRIST

All last night the darkness
was full of writing that I could not read.
It was not written for a crowd
by a tight fit between hand and pen.
Why do we ever think it is?

When my reason has recovered
safer territory, after being overwhelmed
by miracle, O powerful bard,
O humble student, my concrete mind
intends less to control than to discover.

No man can just dip into life
dropping nets and drawing them up.
Leave your nets, for I have found
a good net for a herring fisher,
with unattributed quotations
and abrupt shifts of subjects –

because I am African,
dark, eastern, irrational, non-western,
because I am feminine.

Medbh McGuckian was born in 1950 in Belfast where she still lives and works. She has won the Rooney Prize, the American Ireland Fund Literary Award, England's National Poetry Competition and the Forward Prize for Best Poem. Her first collection was published by Oxford University Press in 1982, and, since 1991, The Gallery Press have published fifteen of her books. *The Unfixed Horizon: New Selected Poems* was published by Wake Forest University Press in 2015, and a new selected poems is underway with The Gallery Press. She is a member of Aosdána.